Rhy
Freedom

*Lots of Love
Wendy
xx*

07899918378 :)

Rhymes of Life Freedom

A guide to having more fun and living without limits

Wendy Dunning

Rhymes of Life

© Wendy Dunning 2013

All rights reserved, no part of this publication may be reproduced, stored or transmitted in any forms, or by any means electronic, except in the case of brief quotations embodied in critical articles and reviews, without the prior permission of the author.

No digital imprints to be copied or shared.
Please respect the intellectual property
and copyright of the author.

Published by Rhymes of Life
www.rhymesoflife.info

An imprint of Rhymes of Life
59 Glebe Road
Hinckley
Leicestershire
LE10 1HF
United Kingdom

ISBN 978-0-9927745-0-9

Illustrations

Thanks

I am grateful to my life partner Paul - for his amazing patience and unfailing, ongoing, loving support. I also acknowledge my dear friends - for their positive attitude and constant encouragement.

A special thanks goes out to my spirit guide - my dragon, for bringing laughter into the creative process. For quietly encouraging and inspiring me every day, in ways I did not know were possible until he led me to them. For allowing me to sit with him, until his boundless wisdom washed over me and the words flowed onto paper.

Thank you to everyone who read my draft rhymes and loved them so much that they ordered a book. Your enthusiasm kept me focused on reaching my goal and getting this into print. I hope you all enjoy reading the rhymes as much as I have enjoyed writing them.

Contents

Chapter	Rhyme	Page
Introduction		9
The Rhymes		19
1.	Creating	20
2.	Foundations	22
3.	Tunnel	24
4.	Seed	26
5.	The Corner	28
6.	Comfort Zone	30
7.	Perfect	32
8.	My Vehicle	34
9.	Now	36
10.	Change	38
11.	Another Way	40
12.	Ruts	42
13.	Train	44
14.	Mountain	46
15.	Lion	48
16.	Puppet	50
17.	Release	52
18.	Director	54
19.	Pedestal	56
20.	Rights	58
21.	Unlock	60
22.	Opening	62
23.	Vows	64
24.	Award	66

25.	Evolving	68
26.	Forgiveness	70
27.	Gratitude	72
28.	Flower	74
29.	Back Pack	76
30.	My Shoes	78
31.	Choices	80
32.	Diamond	82
33.	Roundabout	84
34.	Catch A Star	86
35.	Target	88
36.	Juggling	90
37.	Done	92
38.	Ant	94
39.	Ancestors	96
40.	Listen	98
41.	Heart Talk	100
42.	Words	102
43.	My Truth	104
44.	DNA	106
45.	Water	108
46.	Peace	110
47.	Waking	112
48.	Connecting	114
49.	Armour	116
50.	Ripples	118
51.	Footprints	120
52.	Party	122
The Toolbox		125

Unlock the locks
As you have the key
Remove your old limits
And set yourself free

Introduction

The Book

'Rhymes of Life – Freedom' explores deep wisdom in an amazingly accessible and unique way. You can open a page and enjoy a rhyme, read some more and discover your own beliefs on the subject, or take the ideas and use them to change your life.

The 52 simple and melodic rhymes which form the foundation of this book are like small lights, shining onto the subject of personal freedom, slowly revealing the truth about this fascinating subject.

The opposite pages allow you to stop and gently explore your present thinking, inspiring new and exciting personal discoveries. They offer guidance on how to focus on what you really want and remove blockages and limits that may be holding you back.

The toolbox offers easy, practical, step by step techniques to let go of old, deep, unhealthy patterns and find some new, more useful ways to move forward.

This book is like life, packed full of new and exciting little adventures. So have fun splashing around in its unstoppable positivity and let it carry you downstream, towards your dreams.

Freedom

Freedom is a subject that is so important to us as human beings that we have fought wars in the name of it. Many people have gone into battle and died to establish our individual rights to be free. This is not a book that debates these human rights and their legality; it is a book that suggests that we are not celebrating the freedom so many have fought for, the freedom that we all have available to us right now.

Most of us are not held in prisons of stone and steel, instead we have made walls from our thoughts and bars from our limiting beliefs. We are the ones who locked the doors, we just need the right tools to open them and set ourselves free.

So here is a large selection of keys woven into a book, where every page offers opportunities to take off your shackles and loosen your chains. Some are keys that are new and shiny, some are older ones you will be delighted to rediscover. Among them are keys to power, control, abundance, peace, joy, fun and much, much more. There are keys to keep and keys to share, all of them are positive and useful, all of them open doors that lead towards a happier and healthier life for whoever holds and uses them.

My Story

When I arrived on this planet I thought I owned and controlled the world, like most young children I believed everything was mine. My thoughts and actions were completely spontaneous and utterly free; I cried when I wanted to and did whatever felt right in that moment. I don't exactly remember, but I can imagine, that when people started to say NO! I must have been really puzzled. NO you can't reach that you are too small, NO you can't do that you are not clever enough, NO you can't have that because you are not permitted to touch or own it. Their ideas directly conflicted with mine and led to deep confusion - I could not understand! I thought I was limitless, so what were these big loud people talking about? What did it all mean?

At first I did not believe them. I was sure I could do whatever I felt like doing, so I pushed at my boundaries. I tried climbing and more than once I fell, surprisingly, it hurt. I tried flapping my arms really hard and was shocked to discover that I could not fly. Slowly I began to conclude that maybe I did not know everything, maybe they were right and I was wrong. I began to believe these big clever people who had authority over me.

I now realise that most of what I was told as a small child was intended to keep me safe, to protect me and stop me from exploring in my cute but unlimited way. I was very firmly told 'you can't', 'you mustn't', 'you are too small', 'you are limited', 'I choose for you - you don't get to choose for yourself' and I believed it all.

At that age I was like a little sponge, I absorbed what I heard as if it was all completely true. Sometimes I did not understand what I was being told, but I accepted it anyway. It all went in and somehow it all became rather stuck inside me, like the basic programming of a computer, it was soon deeply fixed in my core. My parents and teachers' beliefs had become my beliefs. I repeated them quietly to myself to help me remember (like my times tables). Before long I knew them so well that they ran completely automatically.

I was naturally curious, so I kept exploring as I grew. I began to decide some things for myself, I developed my own opinion. I occasionally made small changes in my thinking, testing and adapting what I had been taught as a young child. I tried to make my new learning fit or merge with my basic core beliefs but most of the time I found that I was just pasting over the top of what was already there, unable to edit my deepest and most fundamental programming.

With everything I had, I did my best. I went through school, then to work, dated, married and had two children of my own, but I was not happy. I longed for freedom yet I felt small, trapped and powerless. I was no longer a child but with my old thinking and programming I often felt and acted like one.

It seemed as if all the enthusiasm I was born with had been squashed out of me by those comments that I couldn't or shouldn't do what came naturally to me. It felt as if all the excitement I'd had for life as a young child was lost or buried under a pile of ideas that were depressing and negative.

Part of me felt completely stuck. Another part of me knew there had to be another way to live - anything had to be better than this! So I went out into the world and asked questions. I searched for the real answers and the whole truth.

I explored books and courses on psychology, counselling, therapy and self-development. Slowly I began to alter my core programming - I began to adapt and alter my beliefs. I began to make changes, at first reluctantly, then with more and more excitement and enthusiasm.

I slowly began to uncover the truth, to peel back the layers of confusion, to uncover the wisdom that lay below it all.

As I explored, to my wonder and amazement, I began to rediscover what I had instinctively known as a child - that life was not to be feared or avoided, but lived as a great adventure; I started to remember what it felt like to feel powerful and free. I began to push away the boundaries that had been placed on me by others. I carefully removed many of the restrictions and limits I had placed on myself, I changed my thinking and I slowly changed my life.

Now that I realise I really am an adult, now that I realise I am not restricted by people who say that I can't, or I am too small, now that I do not believe the imposed limits of childhood, I have finally woken up to the truth that I am the one in control of my own destiny. I have the right to choose whatever feels true, whatever makes me happy, whatever sets me free.

Writing this book on the subject of personal freedom has given me more time to focus on it, to explore it, to understand it, to study its deeper meanings, to stay in its energy.

I am very thankful to have had the opportunity to investigate freedom and what it means to me. What I have discovered has changed me forever.

I am sharing my discoveries, so you can explore your own barriers to freedom and dissolve away your own blockages.
So you can move forward to explore the positive experiences that I know are waiting for you. I hope it will allow you to make positive and powerful changes, bringing more freedom and joy into every area of your life.

So feel free to take what you want to from what I have written. Discover what feels, sounds or looks right for you as an individual, uncovering your own way to use what you find. Plot a way forward, then take the real and practical steps to reach your own targets. This book offers a variety of keys to assist you, maybe you will choose big keys or begin with the small ones, maybe you will put in a little energy or a lot, maybe you will make the changes in days, months or over years. My hope is that this book will guide you, awakening you to the truth - that you always had the power and freedom to choose your own way to feel and act, the right to choose your own way to live

Maybe you too can reconnect with the freedom and power that you were born with, maybe you too will reclaim your own right to be truly free.

Remember what you came with
Remember what is true
You can release the limits
And choose what's right for you

Using This Book

There is no right or wrong way to use this book.

In my own small way I am letting you know that you are free to find your own individual way to use every page of this book. To choose any section, any phrase or tool as a key to assist your own progress. I actively encourage you to increase your trust in your own intuition, to listen to your gut knowing and follow your heart. So all I ask is that you explore fearlessly and discover what is really true for you.

There are rhymes to read and ideas to explore. There are exercises to try and techniques to use.

If you want to gain more from the wisdom and keys stored here then return to this book regularly. If you want to make the changes deeper or faster use the toolbox. You can have fun with it, dipping in and out, taking from it whatever feels right for you in any moment of any day that you choose to open its pages.

The Rhymes

Creating

What I put in is what I get out
So I'm careful as I choose
Results they always follow
The ingredients I use

Everything I add right now
Tomorrow's joy will make
Even when I do not move
That's still a choice I take

All the actions made today
Bring outcomes back to me
My behaviour is creating
The way my life will be

Explore & Discover

Consider... If you were writing a recipe for happiness, what ingredients would you add to the mixture? What ingredients would you always leave out? How does what you put into today affect the results of tomorrow?

Realise... When we are cooking we often keep to our favorite recipe. Sometimes that is just the easiest thing to do after a long day at work. What we put in and the method we use directly lead to the way our food tastes and looks. By mixing things up, we can always create new and exciting flavours and results. When we put positive, powerful thoughts into anything, we get more positive, powerful results back in return. We can choose the ingredients we use each day, and the results will follow.

Imagine... Having unlimited choices about what you can do today, unlimited ingredients that you might be able to combine in a new way, to create new and exciting results for yourself.

Affirm... What I put in is what I get out - what I choose today creates all my tomorrows.

Foundations

From the time of my birth
I collected what's true
Like bricks in a wall
The old and the new

Some came from my parents
Or times that have passed
And slowly I placed them
Each one on the last

When life pushes hard
And I'm rocked to the core
I stand here and now
On what's laid before

Explore & Discover

Consider... How stable do you feel? How solid are your emotional foundations? Were the people that taught you the basics of life master builders? Are you ready to rebuild your own foundations?

Realise... We began building our foundations when we were small; we took the beliefs and truths offered by the adults around us, and used this as a basic structure to stand and travel on. The quality of our foundations directly influences how stable we feel when the wind blows or life pushes hard. Each time we alter our core beliefs, replacing them with something sturdier and more powerful, we are replacing old bricks with new stronger ones, rebuilding the foundations that will support us through the rest of our life.

Imagine... A future where you stand tall and proud, where your foundations all fit together perfectly, giving you strength and stability so that nothing ever knocks you off balance again.

Affirm... My foundations are strong and stable - I choose balance right now.

Tunnel

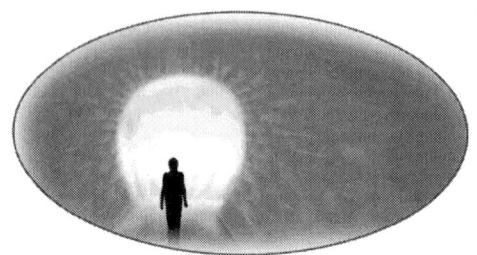

When I am in dark places
And it is hard to see
Then looking at the walls
Will never set me free

If I focus on the light
Then that will lead the way
Towards a bright tomorrow
From the darkness of today

So I will count my blessings
However black it seems
I'll move out of the tunnel
And walk into my dreams

Explore & Discover

Consider... When you feel trapped or in a dark tunnel do you focus on the darkness or the light? Do you spend more time focused on problems or exploring possible solutions? If you focused on the light at the end of the tunnel, would you be more likely to move towards it?

Realise... When we feel that we are in a tunnel or dark place, we might only be aware of the darkness around us. When we change our focus we may notice that there is always a way out. When we give our time and attention to the light and positive things in our life, we automatically take steps in that direction. Bit by bit, step by step we move forward. As the darkness fades away we arrive in the brightest light and most wonderful experiences.

Imagine... Walking right into the light at the end of a dark tunnel - use your amazing imagination to explore the world that you find. Turn up the enthusiasm and excitement, make it bright and perfect for you.

Affirm... The light is always there waiting - I choose to take real and practical steps towards it now.

Seed

Every seed that's planted
It wants the world to know
That it is pure potential
And put on earth to grow

It moves out from the darkness
Its dreams are big and bright
It knows it has a purpose
It turns towards the light

It grows with every cycle
Gets stronger every day
Through all the storms and sunshine
It bends and finds a way

Explore & Discover

Consider... Are you heading towards brighter days, full of happiness and success? Are you willing to push through the dark earth and challenging storms to reach your goals? What would happen if you followed your instinct, turned towards the light, stretched and moved steadily upwards, growing stronger with every day that passed?

Realise... Each seed is pure potential. It does not analyse or think about how to grow; it trusts its instincts and always heads towards the light. With enough nourishment it will become what it is meant to be, a flower, a fruit or a huge tree. We all have a purpose here on Earth. When we listen to our instincts, they guide us to find and embrace it.

Imagine... Noticing your biggest and brightest dreams and turning towards them, trusting your instinctive desire to align with them. Welcoming the rain and the sunshine, which help you to grow and become everything you were meant to be.

Affirm... I am exploring and evolving. I discover a little more with each sunrise.

The Corner

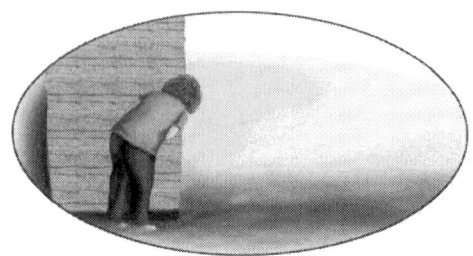

Its fear that holds me back
From dreams I never dared
I worry and avoid
The truth is I am scared

But I can choose again
And find another way
I'll trust myself to cope
With my challenges today

I simply do my best
And let each moment come
Whatever's round the corner
I will smile and make it fun

Explore & Discover

Consider... Do you spend time and energy worrying about things that may never happen? Do you believe you can cope with whatever challenges lie ahead? What would be different if you looked forward to what was around the corner with curiosity and enthusiasm?

Realise... Life is always bringing us new challenges and surprises; they are always just around the corner. We can choose to look forward to them with dread or with excitement. This won't change what happens later today, or tomorrow, but it might alter how much fun we are having right now. Everything becomes easier when we trust ourselves to survive and handle what is coming next.

Imagine... Peering around the corner with excitement rather than concern, looking forward to whatever comes next. Imagine having the power, self-belief and confidence to cope with all of life's challenges, to enjoy the adventures that are out of sight just around the corner.

Affirm... I coped yesterday - I am coping now - I will cope with whatever comes next.

Comfort Zone

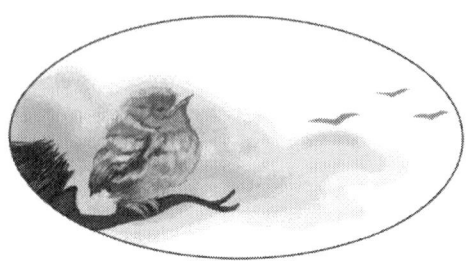

Just like a baby bird
Who's wings have never flown
My freedom can be found
Outside my comfort zone

So when I take a chance
And try out the unknown
My dreams can all be reached
Outside my comfort zone

When I take a leap of faith
And set off on my own
There's a whole world waiting
Outside my comfort zone

Explore & Discover

Consider... Do you stay inside the comfort zone of what you have already experienced? Is your comfort zone a safe place or somewhere that stops you from flying around and having fun?

Realise... We all have an instinctive fear of the unknown; we often prefer to keep within the limits of what we already know. We may avoid anything that threatens to move us out of our safe, cosy places and habits. Just like a baby bird, sometimes we might prefer to stay in the nest and be fed by our parents, even if it limits our freedom. A bird is created with wings so it can be free to fly. Maybe freedom is waiting for us - when we trust ourselves enough to take a leap of faith into the unknown and explore the world outside of our own comfort zone.

Imagine... The world that is waiting for you when you grab your courage, push your fears aside, let go of old limits and fly outside your comfort zone.

Affirm... I summon all my courage and take a leap of faith - outside my comfort zone and into freedom.

Perfect

It doesn't have to be perfect
For nothing ever is
Life is an adventure
It never was a quiz

It doesn't have to be perfect
For I've realised what's true
Through each event I'm learning
My best will have to do

It doesn't have to be perfect
For a moment or a day
And all that stand in judgment
Must know it works that way

Explore & Discover

Consider... Do you expect yourself to get everything right? Who decides what is right and wrong - who is making the rules? Do you want to be perfect? How many perfect people have you met in your life? Are imperfections normal and acceptable for human beings?

Realise... Our parents wanted us to be happy and healthy. They wanted to teach us how to be as good, or maybe even better than them. However they were not perfect themselves so they could not teach us how to be flawless. Our parents were imperfect, our partners and friends are imperfect, I am imperfect, you are also imperfect. If you look around, you may realise that human beings are designed that way. In human beings imperfections are to be expected - they are absolutely perfect.

Imagine... A world where no one expects perfection, a world where we all accept the flaws of others - and ourselves.

Affirm... I am perfect just as I am - with all my beautiful imperfections.

My Vehicle

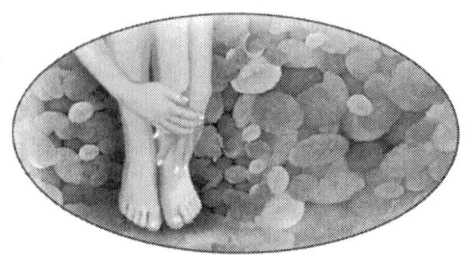

I'm grateful for my hands
And what they let me do
My body is so perfect
For this world I'm walking through

I appreciate each cell
It simply does its best
It takes the actions that I choose
To work and play then rest

With care it keeps on moving
I keep it fit and strong
Each day I thank this vehicle
As it carries me along

Explore & Discover

Consider... Do you appreciate the vehicle that carries you through your life? Do you give it good fuel, keep it clean and service it regularly? If it stops working do you pay to get it fixed and back on the road quickly? What is your vehicle, your body, worth to you?

Realise... Some people spend more time and money on keeping their car running than their own body. Our bodies are mostly self-repairing, but without proper care they can stop working. This vehicle is our transport for a lifetime. If it does not work well this can limit our freedom of movement. When we put in good fuel, keeping it healthy and in balance, it rewards us by running smoothly and taking us in any direction that we choose to go.

Imagine... Slowly looking at each part of your body in turn, thanking it aloud for what it has done to help you travel through your life. Send it some love and appreciation.

Affirm... This is my own unique body. I love, accept and appreciate every cell - it is simply amazing.

Now

When I look at my past
Stories kept for so long
I cannot go back
And fix what went wrong

When I gaze at the future
And dream what might be
My hopes and my worries
They are just fantasy

When I'm here in the present
All time can align
In this moment of power
All choices are mine

Explore & Discover

Consider... Do you spend time and energy wishing you could go back and change the past? Do you worry about a future that may never even arrive? Do you enjoy each moment that comes and goes? Do you live in the past, present or future? How simple would your life be if you lived in the now?

Realise... The past is really gone - even if it is not forgotten. The future is all our hopes, dreams, fears and worries, but we cannot live in tomorrow as it is only today when we live and breathe. Maybe the only time that is real is the moment we are standing or sitting in - right here, right now. Perhaps this is our time of choice and power.

Imagine... Letting go of your dreams about the future and living fully in the present moment. Slow down your thoughts and focus on what is actually happening now, appreciate everything, really stop to smell the roses, full of gratitude for all the blessings and gifts of this moment and this day.

Affirm... I am choosing to stop and appreciate this moment and this breath.

Change

I can change when I want to
I can change what I do
I can alter my habits
I know that it's true

So I'll keep what is working
And change what is not
If I want big changes
Then I'll change a lot

I will put in the effort
I will make the work fun
I'll rest and relax
When the changes are done

Explore & Discover

Consider... Do you welcome or avoid change? Do you hold on tight to what you have, or adapt to what presents itself each day? Are you prepared to let go of habits that are not working for you? Could you - would you - will you change?

Realise... Change is a natural process and to avoid it we must resist time and life itself. We cannot stop change but we can take control of our own changes by making more conscious and focused choices. We can stay stuck or we can move on, we can hold tight or let go, we can stay the same or change any part of our life, we can make the changes a struggle or relax and enjoy them. When we recognise our own freedom to change and to choose, then we take back the power to transform our own lives.

Imagine... Being in a future where you have reached your dreams - take some time to really see, feel and hear what happens in that possible dreamy future. What personal changes will you make to reach these dreams?

Affirm... I am taking control of the changes and choosing for me.

Another Way

It's time to change what doesn't work
Old patterns cannot stay
Whatever does not bring me joy
I'll find another way

So watch me alter what I do
Listen to what I say
Nothing lasts for ever
So I choose another way

I believe in living free
With all I am today
I'm following my heart this time
There is always another way

Explore & Discover

Consider... Where is your life heading? What do you do just because you have always done it that way? Do you have the courage to explore new routines and take your life in a new direction? Could a small adjustment today make a large difference down the road?

Realise... We all run strategies and routines - we run these procedures for everything, from getting dressed in the morning to how we shop. When we started doing them they seemed like the obvious and best thing to do, but that was then - and this is now - and now we have many more choices available. Every small positive change we make today is like a fork in our road, allowing us to reach a much better destination at some point in the future.

Imagine... Focusing on one thing in your life that is not working, writing down all the things you could do to make changes, then trying your ideas until you find something that really works for you.

Affirm... If something doesn't work today, I will choose another way.

Ruts

I've travelled here for many years
With habits that I keep
The steps I take are forming dips
My ruts are getting deep

It sometimes seems much easier
To do the things I've done
But maybe there's another way
Where I can have more fun

I know that there's a world out there
And now it's time to move
I choose freedom every time
I step out of this groove

Explore & Discover

Consider... Do you act unconsciously or consciously? Are you stuck in a rut – addicted to what you know? Will your ruts get you where you want to go?

Realise... That we can only think about a few things consciously at one time, so we run most of our thoughts and actions unconsciously. Repeating what we know is easy and creates habits; soon we find we have made grooves in our road. With a little effort we can slowly move out of old unhealthy ruts, consciously explore all our possible options and make more positive, powerful healthy choices.

Imagine... A world where here are no habits or ruts, where everyone decides everything based on what is best for them in each moment. Imagine becoming aware of all your old patterns and consciously choosing to let go of old unhealthy routines. Could you step out of your old habits and grooves to make some new healthy ones?

Affirm... I am consciously choosing my thoughts and actions now – my actions are creating some new and very exciting grooves.

Train

I am clearing the rails
I am not looking back
It's time to move forward
Get the snow off the track

I am giving permission
So the barriers raise
Then onward I travel
With power and praise

I am changing the signals
They are old and untrue
Move out of the way
For I'm coming through

Explore & Discover

Consider... What are your biggest barriers to freedom and joy? Do you give up at the first obstacle or try, try and try again? Are you focused, determined and courageous enough to push through and travel on?

Realise... Our ability to accept unlimited freedom is often based on our old limiting beliefs. If we are holding ourselves back then we also have the power to change the signals and let ourselves go. If we put down fear and pick up courage, if we are determined, if we never give up trying, then the world will move aside, as we push through all the barriers to reach success and happiness.

Imagine... Deciding on a personal goal that you want to reach, then noticing that it has a train track which leads towards it. Then using your amazing imagination to slowly and deliberately clear your own way forward, imagine using a snow plough, sweeping brush or anything else that allows you to reach your desired target more easily.

Affirm... Let the barriers raise - I am moving ahead right now.

Mountain

Maybe it's a mountain
The task that lies ahead
Maybe it's a molehill
And really small instead

Maybe it takes years and years
Or minutes to be done
Maybe it is really hard
Or I could make it fun

Maybe I am really stuck
Or I could start today
Maybe it's just my fears
That are standing in my way

Explore & Discover

Consider... Do you ever make mountains out of molehills? Do you ever get anxious about doing something then feed it with your fear until it grows larger and scarier? Is what you fear real or just your imagination working overtime? What mountains could you climb if you were completely fearless?

Realise... A small task (a molehill) can easily become much larger (a mountain) if we feed it our fear. Common fears that stop us are the fear of failure or the fear of getting it 'wrong'. Some people are even afraid of success. Many of our fears are not rational and are based on false beliefs. When we let go of fear everything is more exciting and fun.

Imagine... Sitting quietly and dropping your attention to your chest, then making a list of your fears by finishing the statement, 'I am afraid of...' Then write down their opposites. 'I am not afraid of...' Sit quietly with each item on the second list and repeat each phrase on it ten times.

Affirm... I choose fearless thoughts and fearless actions - I am fearless now.

Lion

Today I'm a lion
With courage to spare
Powerful and fearless
With long golden hair

Today I'm a lion
And I deserve more
I don't need to tiptoe
Instead I just roar

I take on the energy
I just breathe it in
Today I'm a lion
Let the wildness begin

Explore & Discover

Consider... Do you have timid, fearful thoughts - or brave and adventurous ones? What could you do if you had the courage of a lion? Would life be more fun if you were more wild and courageous today?

Realise... No one ever told lions they shouldn't roar. No one told any of them not to go for whatever they wanted. No one shamed or embarrassed them. Lions don't use words, they trust their instincts. Lions are wild and free and proud of it. Maybe it is time to be more like a lion. With some wild and free ideas, we can have more wild and free thoughts and feelings, followed by more wild and free actions in every area of our lives.

Imagine... A courageous, confident, powerful, fearless yet friendly lion. Take in a few deep breaths as you slowly breathe in its energy. Imagine its power flowing into your heart centre in the middle of your chest, then overflowing from there all around your body, filling every cell, until you are full of unlimited lion courage and confidence.

Affirm... I will never give in - let the wildness begin.

Puppet

I'm not a puppet
For now I am grown
I'm cutting the cords
I can dance on my own

So thanks for the guidance
I've come a long way
You cannot control me
For today's a new day

The old stage has ended
And a new one is here
I choose my own moves
I'm my own puppeteer

Explore & Discover

Consider... Have you been a puppet? Who has been pulling your strings? Can you take action on your own without puppet masters? Can you walk forward or dance choosing your own free and unrestricted moves?

Realise... Our connections to people from the past can hold us down or back, stopping us from moving forward freely. When we stay connected they still have the power to control us, to push our buttons and pull our strings. If we hold onto them, we are keeping them in our lives. When we let them go we set ourselves free.

Imagine... Noticing your connection to someone from your past that you would like to release. Take time to imagine the cords or energy connections that keep you both attached. Imagine the colour and any other details about these cords, notice their width and direction of flow. Use your amazing imagination to alter or cut them in a way that feels right for you. Thank them for all the good times and let them go.

Affirm... I choose to release what no longer serves me - I cut the ties and set myself free.

Release

I break the old patterns
My chains to the past
Release expectations
So I'm free at last

I am so grateful
For what came before
But this is my time
And now I want more

I take back my power
To choose my own way
Now I am deciding
What I do today

Explore & Discover

Consider... Who decides what you do? Do you believe you *should* or *ought* to do things, although they do not feel comfortable or natural to you? Do you feel that you *need* to act a certain way? Can you break the chains to cultural or family rules about how you should live your life and choose your own path to happiness?

Realise.... We are often taught there are certain things we *need* to do, but there is nothing we really *need* to do. We do not have to follow anyone else's rules. We can consider our options, weigh up the consequences of each choice and decide what we want to do today.

Imagine... Making a list of all the things in your life that you believe you *need* to do e.g. I need to go shopping - then re-writing your list swapping the word *need* for *choose*, e.g. I choose to go shopping. Consider which statements are really true for you. Notice how your enthusiasm changes when you make this simple change in your language.

Affirm... There is nothing I *need* to do - I am choosing it all.

Director

I came to walk upon this stage
I choose each act I take
Direct myself to move and speak
With every thought I make

My actions are what I control
And others choose their way
Together we weave storylines
With the parts we've come to play

Actors come and actors go
Each day is here then gone
Years they past—the earth it turns
The show it carries on

Explore & Discover

Consider... If the whole world is a stage, what part of it are you directing? How much time and energy do you use trying to direct other people and how much do you use taking command of your own life? What scenes would you choose if you took back the power to be your own director?

Realise... We have complete control over what we choose to think, feel and do. Other people are their own directors - they make their own decisions, which create their own positive or negative results. Trying to direct other people always leads to frustration and disappointment as they are beyond our control. We each choose our own role in the play of life; the show continuously unfolds because every person plays their part so beautifully.

Imagine... Taking a few steps back to sit in the director's chair of your life. What do you notice from that position that you have not seen before? What calm and kind advice or direction could you give to yourself?

Affirm... I choose my actions today; I am the director of my own life.

Pedestal

When I do not choose
With my power inside
I raise up the others
As I let them decide

When I know I have value
Then the pedestals fall
No need to be better
No need to play small

As we are all equal
No one has more worth
We all live and breath
As we stand on the earth

Explore & Discover

Consider... Have you noticed people putting others down so that they can feel more powerful and important? Do you play small or big? Do you take energy and power from others? Do you give your own power away? What could you do if you took your own power back and felt powerful?

Realise... We are all born with equal rights, power and control over our own lives. If we were told we were more important than others, or if we were told we were less valuable than anyone else, this may not be true. We have our own power centre inside us. If we gave our power away, we can also choose to take it back, to return it to where it belongs.

Imagine... Focusing on the middle of your chest. Imagine that this is your own internal power centre, which contains a powerful magnet that can easily pull back any power which you gave away in the past. Allow it to flow back like energy - into your chest until you feel powerful.

Affirm... I am naturally powerful today and every day.

Rights

On the day I was born
My human rights came
So show me respect now
And I'll do the same

My time it is precious
I know what I'm worth
We all deserve honour
As we walk on this earth

I make my decisions
Choose what's right for me
I live without limits
I'm already free

Explore & Discover

Consider... Do you know your human rights? Do you live as though you have the right to think in your own way and express your own opinions? Do you know your own true value and worth? Do you allow yourself all the freedom that is clearly and naturally yours?

Realise... All human beings are born free and equal in dignity and rights. We are entitled to life, liberty and the pursuit of happiness. This is so important to us as a society that we have created laws to uphold these basic human rights for everyone in the world. We all have freedom to choose our own beliefs and choices, to share our ideas and be respected for who we are as individuals. When we fully recognise and honour ourselves and our own rights, we start a wave of loving respect that ripples out, reaching our friends, families and the wider world.

Imagine... A world where every individual human being is treated with unlimited honour and respect for being who they are.

Affirm... I love, value and respect myself - I honour my right to be free and happy today.

Unlock

I was the judge
And the jury as well
I said I was guilty
And locked up my cell

I've been punished enough
For mistakes that I made
The sentence is over
I think that I've paid

I unlock the locks
As I have the key
Forgiving the past
I now set myself free

Explore & Discover

Consider... Were you taught right from wrong and that wrongdoing would be punished? Were your parents and teachers always right themselves? Are you punishing yourself for your own mistakes? Who has locked you up and who holds the key to release you?

Realise... When we feel guilty we can become our own judge and jury; deciding what punishment we deserve for not always knowing or understanding what we recently realised. If we are our own jailors, then we hold the keys to our own freedom. Acceptance and forgiveness are the keys to set us free from guilt, when we forgive ourselves we open the doors to abundance, joy and success in every area of our lives.

Imagine... A key to your freedom - close your eyes and really make it something special, magical, beautiful and perfect for you. Imagine unlocking locks as you say aloud, 'I choose freedom today - I forgive myself and I set myself free'.

Affirm... I accept and forgive all my human flaws - I set myself free now.

Opening

I deserve success
No sabotage for me
I'm taking off the limits
I've decided I am free

I deserve the joy
A world of pure delight
Now I'm always choosing
To make my future bright

I deserve it all
I let abundance flow
The gifts of life are welcome
I breathe—I learn—I grow

Explore & Discover

Consider... Do you set limits on what you deserve? Is there a part of you that sabotages your own happiness, joy or success? Do you really believe that you are worthy of all the wonderful gifts that life has to offer? What could you do if you were open to unlimited abundance and joy today?

Realise... Our limiting beliefs create real limits. If we have made vows never to be really happy, if we feel guilty and want to punish ourselves, if we believe we only deserve a certain level of happiness, freedom or personal power, we will find a way to make this what we receive. As we change our self-worth we open doors to new possibilities and opportunities to receive.

Imagine... A set of dials - one each for your joy, trust, happiness, power, love, peace, freedom, abundance, confidence, self-acceptance and success. Imagine noticing and writing down their present setting levels - from 1-10, then imagine slowly and deliberately turning them all up much, much higher.

Affirm... I am taking off the limits - my arms are open wide to receive all the blessings of life.

Vows

At great turning points
In my own history
I made some oaths
Of how things would be

I promised forever
I swore what I'd do
In that moment I meant it
That day it was true

If I cannot keep it
I'll let it go now
With every step forward
I make a new vow

Explore & Discover

Consider... When you make promises do you mean to keep them? If you made a promise or vow today, can you guarantee you will be able to keep it every day for the rest of your life? Does everyone around you always manage to keep all their promises and vows?

Realise... Most people plan to keep their promises, but discover that what was vowed at some point in the past, is not always true or possible today. Everything changes: situations change, relationships change, people change. Maybe our expectations of others and ourselves are not always realistic. Maybe today is the only day we can really decide what we are capable of and what we are comfortable feeling or doing.

Imagine.... Writing down a list of statements that begin, 'I will always...' or 'I will never...' Then slowly going through them, checking if they are possible and right for whom you are today. Do they make you feel free and happy, or would these vows be better if they were rewritten to fit the situation that you are in now?

Affirm... I vow to love and accept what is.

Award

Each effort I am making
The others do not see
The only one that's watching
And listening is me

I'll give myself a medal
For what I've done so far
If I was only little
I'd give myself a star

I'm proud of each achievement
I'm searching out new ways
To celebrate my actions
By turning up the praise

Explore & Discover

Consider... When you were small were you told that what you did was not good enough - maybe never good enough? Did your parents have high expectorations of you? Were you given lots of praise so that you were rewarded for all your efforts? Do you judge yourself harshly now or turn up the praise and pat yourself on the back?

Realise... Parents want their children to succeed so they often share the expectations of their society, culture or family. Some of these expectations can be unrealistic. Maybe it is time to put down expectations and pick up praise. Sometimes we are the only people that notice our own achievements. Our greatest motivator is the praise we give ourselves; it encourages us to do more and more, to gain in confidence and walk with our head held high.

Imagine... Appreciating everything that you do, everything you try, every effort you make, every small or large personal challenge you overcome.

Affirm... I let go of my expectations - I choose to appreciate every effort that I make.

Evolving

Time and seasons pass on by
I watch each dawn arrive
My breath and body let me know
I'm here and I'm alive

I have come to grow and learn
In any way I can
Evolution never stops
It's part of nature's plan

The world it spirals out and on
As slowly round I go
I just surrender to it all
I'm living in the flow

Explore & Discover

Consider... Do you appreciate how far you have come, how much you have evolved during this lifetime? Are you the same person you were ten years ago, or have you changed? Are you still learning, growing and evolving?

Realise... As time and seasons pass, everything changes. Harder things like rocks change more slowly, softer things like people, animals and plants change more quickly. The world turns, and humanity evolves. It is like a spiraling seashell which always pushes beyond established boundaries, moving around and growing out. Human beings are getting taller, living longer, changing and developing in many different ways. Along with the rest of the human race we are constantly adapting to an ever changing world of new and exciting possibilities.

Imagine... Stepping away from the earth and looking kindly at your own personal growth from a distance. How far have you come? What is the next step in your evolution?

Affirm... Everything is unfolding perfectly - I am simply evolving.

Forgiveness

I drop my expectations
I simply let them fall
I do not sit in judgment
I just accept it all

The anger and frustration
It's time to set them free
I do not want to hold them
They are not good for me

Instead I choose acceptance
I'm thankful for each day
I will enjoy the moment
Whatever comes my way

Explore & Discover

Consider... Do you have high expectations of others? Do you have even higher expectations of yourself? If you could choose judgment and holding on or acceptance and letting go, which would you choose? Can you, do you, will you forgive and move on?

Realise... When we hold on to expectations, anger and bitterness, we are holding onto something very toxic. Holding on does not protect us and it does not punish the other people involved. It is like keeping poison inside us, which affects our minds and bodies. When we forgive others we let go of expectations and fill ourselves with more acceptance, peace and love. When we forgive ourselves we set ourselves free on every level, this can bring us positive improvements in every area of our life.

Imagine... A future where there is no judgment or expectations - just lots of encouragement when someone stumbles and makes a mistake. Where everyone understands and everyone forgives, where people are accepted with all their human flaws.

Affirm... I accept - I forgive - I love my imperfections.

Gratitude

I'm grateful for the beauty
For all I feel and see
The natural world I live in
The peaceful flower and tree

I'm grateful for support
A hug to show you care
For gentleness and kindness
Each moment that we share

I'm grateful for my life
And every breath I take
I stop and thank it all
With every step I make

Explore & Discover

Consider... Do you spend more time complaining about what you do not have in your life - or celebrating what you do have? Do you appreciate all the jewels and treasures that are yours? Have you counted your blessings lately?

Realise... We can choose to notice what is missing from our lives - to always expect more than we have right now, leading to frustration and disappointment. We can choose to be thankful for all the good things we have today. When we stop and count our blessings, we often find there are hidden diamonds and pearls scattered throughout our lives.

Imagine... Stopping each day to count your blessings, maybe writing them down in a book, beginning each line with the words, 'I am grateful for...' Write the smaller things you are thankful for - as well as the larger ones. (Once you start it can be difficult to stop, so just enjoy it and keep going and going.) You are truly blessed.

Affirm... I am grateful for it all - thank you.

Flower

There's no right way to learn
There's no right way to grow
I've checked with the flowers
For all of them know

They just do their best
To grow and be strong
There's no one that judges
If they're getting it wrong

They change and adapt
As the seasons spin by
No worry or pressure
It's enough just to try

Explore & Discover

Consider... What does success mean to you? Is it money or happiness? Are flowers successful? What can we learn from plants and animals about relaxing and being happy?

Realise... That the purpose of every flower's life is to grow, to try any way it can to explore a little more each day. It is determined to thrive throughout all the challenges that life brings. Its greatest desire is to be the best in any way it can. Flowers know all of this - they know that if they turn up to life and play their part in some way, they are doing well just by existing. Human beings are considered to be the more evolved beings, yet many of the flowers seem to be happier than we are - maybe we can gain more wisdom and understanding by watching and appreciating them.

Imagine... Living life with the simplicity of a flower or a tree. Having no worries or expectations, just being happy in the moment, enjoying existing and doing your best.

Affirm... I am a human who is being - a human be-ing. In every moment, it is enough just to be.

Back Pack

All that I've carried
All the worries and fears
Has made me move slowly
For so many years

I'll take off the backpack
And have a look in
I'll sort out the rubbish
And fill up the bin

I'll keep what's important
Whatever feels right
Let go of the baggage
And just travel light

Explore & Discover

Consider... How much old baggage do you carry with you? Is it all useful to you today? If you sorted through what you are carrying, how much would you decide to keep and how much would you choose to throw away? Could you travel lighter?

Realise... When something happens which we cannot fully process, we keep that memory. We often hold on tight and retell stories that have been forgotten by the others involved. Old hurts, frustrations, expectations and other painful memories are heavy and even toxic to carry. When we sort out our old baggage and throw some away, we become lighter and all our movements become much easier.

Imagine... Taking off your own imaginary backpack, putting it down and looking through it. If there is too much to sort through alone, you may wish to find a therapist or use a self-help method. Imagine how you would feel without any heavy, negative memories slowing you down.

Affirm... I am letting go of whatever does not serve me - I only keep positive thoughts and memories now.

My Shoes

This is my body and these are my shoes
I chose to travel this way
I've come so far and worn them well
In the feet I have today

This is my journey and this is my life
With every breath I've grown
I walk my path from birth to death
In a shell that's mine alone

So many paths run parallel
As I share company
But no one shoes are quite like mine
Each steps unique to me

Explore & Discover

Consider... Do you walk your own way? If you walked in someone else's shoes would you walk their way? Do you have the right to walk any way you want to as you take your own personal journey through life?

Realise... We all have an individual life journey to make, following our own distinctive path with unique experiences and purpose. Others may travel on a parallel path to us on their own journeys, but they cannot travel our path and we cannot travel theirs. Expecting others to act, think or feel the same as us will always lead to frustration and disappointment as we are all different. Maybe there is no right or wrong way to take a journey; there is just the way that we choose to travel along our own path today.

Imagine... Looking back at your life journey, soften your eyes, look lovingly and kindly at the path you have taken. Appreciate each achievement, accept that each decision was made with what you understood at that particular time, you were always doing your best.

Affirm... This is my journey - it is as unique as I am.

Choices

There are so many choices
And adventures ahead
Shall I open the green door
Or maybe the red

Each day brings new chances
And fun things to do
With strength and with courage
I will step on through

I'll walk on the wild side
I'll dance in the rain
Find what makes me happy
And drink pink champagne

Explore & Discover

Consider... Do you find new opportunities scary or exciting? Do you look forward to opening new doors or try to stay still for as long as possible to avoid change? Do you allow old doors to close so new ones can open? What exciting adventures might be waiting if you have the courage to open some new doors and step through them?

Realise... As children we are sometimes told we cannot cope with or handle awkward situations. As adults we have already coped with many life challenges. Adults can work, drive, cook, handle sharp scissors or knives, etc., etc. Any child would be seriously impressed. Every door that we close to the past gives us the ability to focus on something new. Doors are always opening in front of us and closing behind us as we move forward, exploring whatever comes next.

Imagine... Many doors ahead, with new experiences waiting behind them. Opening the doors, exploring and trying what comes next to decide if you might like it.

Affirm... I am closing negative doors to the past and opening positive doors to the future.

Diamond

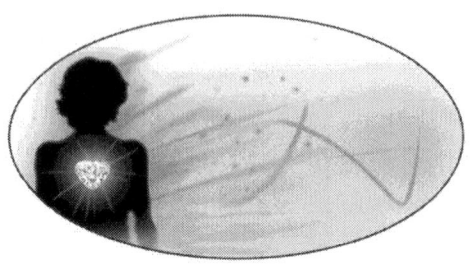

Where the heaviest weight
And pressure is found
There is a treasure
Found deep underground

The burdens upon it
Form a stone clear and bright
A beautiful diamond
That shines in the light

Deep in each heart
There's a jewel pure and fine
Each struggle and challenge
Just help it to shine

Explore & Discover

Consider... Have your past difficulties weakened or strengthened you? Have you learnt more during easy times or when life was full of challenges? Is your inner diamond stronger for the struggles you have overcome?

Realise... Everything that we experience has made us who we are right now. Whether we have taken an easy path or a more difficult one, it has brought us to this moment. We often learn the most from our most difficult struggles and challenges. Maybe we all have our own inner diamond, a pure jewel that is shining inside us, becoming stronger and more powerful as we overcome life's trials.

Imagine... The pure diamond within you that has been created by your struggles. If it is covered with dirt or rubbish maybe it is time to use your imagination to clear that away, allowing it to shine out into the world.

Affirm... I have grown through every challenge – my inner diamond shines and lights up my world.

Roundabout

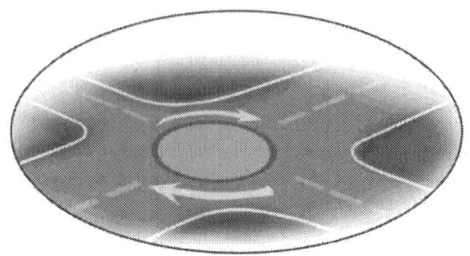

Sometimes I go round and round
As I don't know what to do
There are many roads ahead
And every one is new

It's time to stop and make a choice
It's time to move along
I'll choose with all I know right now
I cannot get it wrong

As I journey through today
I find to my surprise
Another junction soon appears
Right there before my eyes

Explore & Discover

Consider... What do you do if you miss a turn as you travel on your life's journey? What would you do if this happened when you were driving? Would you stop in a lay-by and beat yourself up? Could you simply take the next junction that leads in a powerful, positive direction?

Recognise... We have many choices and junctions on our path each and every day. At each junction we decide which way to go with all we know in that moment and then we move forward down that path. In life our vehicle does not have a reverse gear. We cannot take it backwards in time, however we always have more choices, junctions and possibilities ahead of us than we realise from our present position.

Imagine... That you are on a roundabout now and can take any road that you choose. Imagine looking down all of the roads ahead of you, to consider where you might end up in few years' time.

Affirm... I am getting off the roundabout – I am moving ahead with courage and confidence today.

Catch A Star

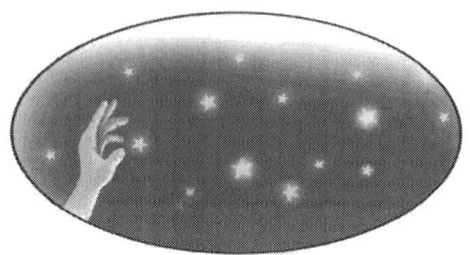

I'm dreaming big and limitless
Imagining I'm free
There is nothing I can't do
When I believe in me

Thinking small is in the past
Little goals won't do
I focus on amazing dreams
And let them all come true

I might just touch the stars today
I might decide to fly
Or brush against an angels wings
While I'm reaching for the sky

Explore & Discover

Consider... How big are your dreams? Do you limit what is possible because you were told you were too stupid, small or immature? What could you have if you believed you none of that was true and you deserved it all now? If your dreams were huge and you reached for enough stars, could you catch a few?

Realise... The limits we had as children are not the same as the limits we have as adults. Whatever we believe is possible for us now sets very real restrictions on our joy, happiness, love, freedom and power. If we reach for a stone, we will soon have a great collection of stones. If we take off our old limits and reach higher, then we have more chances of catching stars and touching rainbows.

Imagine... Living without the limiting beliefs you have collected from the past. Reaching for the biggest, highest, most amazing goals you can imagine. Believing that anything is possible - as maybe - it is!

Affirm... I release all old limits and believe in myself - I am amazing and anything is possible now.

Target

When I want to hit a target
Or gain the winners prize
I concentrate on the central goal
And focus both my eyes

I decide where I am heading
So I know what to do
I look ahead so clearly
The arrow follows through

With practice it gets easy
New habits come my way
My aim is always guiding
What I will reach today

Explore & Discover

Consider... Do you have things you still want to achieve in your life? What are your daydreams. What targets are you aiming for at the moment? What could happen if you chose new targets, then focused your time and energy on hitting or achieving them?

Realise... The first step to making a dream come true is to have a dream; the second is to write it down. The next is to put time and energy into taking the small, practical steps that allow us to reach it. Regular reviews and rewards acknowledge any positive changes we have made. The only difference between dreams and reality is what actions we take.

Imagine... An amazing and exciting dream you would like to come true, which you then write down. Consider and then list the steps to reaching it, setting a realistic time frame for each step. It is easier to hit any target when we know where we are aiming – with persistence and practice everything gets easier and more comfortable.

Affirm... I focus my aim on a target and take one courageous action to reach it today.

Juggling

Every day I juggle
With tasks up in the air
Life's too short for all this stuff
I cannot keep them there

I think I'll have a sort out
As my arms they really ache
Or one day I'll drop the lot
And something's sure to break

I'll choose what is important
Give time to what is mine
If others say please juggle this
I'll smile and then decline

Explore & Discover

Consider... Are you an experienced juggler of tasks? Roughly how many balls do you keep in the air on a daily basis? Are they all really yours - or have you just taken them because no one else picked them up? Could you return some to their rightful owners so they can improve their own juggling skills?

Realise... Each day we choose how we spend our own time and energy. When we decide to take on a new interest, hobby or task it is like picking up a new ball to juggle. Too many balls in the air at once may bring them, or even us, crashing down. Sorting through and prioritising what is really important to us, puts us back in control of our lives. Giving responsibility back to others gives everyone a chance to be a better juggler.

Imagine... Making a list of all the tasks you complete each day and then a list of what you would like to do if you had more time - decide what to put down, give back, pick up or keep juggling.

Affirm... I choose which balls I pick up, put down or keep in the air. My hands, my body, my time, my choice.

Done

I wait for others to hold my hand
I wait for a time that's right
Today is here - it's time to act
To turn on the green light

I'll grab my courage then make a list
I'll stamp each task complete
Glad I put the effort in
Achieving tastes so sweet

When it is finished I look back
I chose and did my best
My confidence is growing now
I'm seriously impressed

Explore & Discover

Consider... Do you wait for others before taking action? Have you been waiting for the right time to move forward? What have you been putting off that you could easily complete? How would you feel if everything that you have been avoiding was done?

Realise... Incomplete tasks can cause barriers and blocks to our progress. They get in our way, impede us and drain our energy, sometimes causing frustration and guilt. A completed task often brings a sense of achievement, motivating us to do more. Each job that is finished moves from in front of us, to behind us; this clears the route ahead. If we complete one thing we have been avoiding each day, the future soon appears brighter and clearer.

Imagine... Listing the tasks you want completed, then doing the one you have been avoiding for the longest (asking others for support if it is difficult to do). Tick it off, pat yourself on the back, reward yourself for your efforts and then move onto the next one until everything is up to date.

Affirm... I believe in myself – I can easily handle this!

Ant

Today I'm an ant
Determined and strong
I believe that I can
So each task won't take long

Today I'm an ant
That is how I win
I just try other ways
And I never give in

Today I'm an ant
Although I am small
I will gather my friends
And push over that wall

Explore & Discover

Consider... Were you taught you were to too small to achieve your dreams? Can you be like an ant, small yet strong and determined to succeed? When a task is too big to complete alone, can you gather your friends and family and complete it together?

Realise... Ants are much smaller than us, but they sometimes have some very big ideas; they do not believe that their size limits their movements. They will climb a tree using tiny steps or move a mountain grain-by-grain. They are team players, prepared to form alliances and join with others to reach their biggest goals. If they meet an obstacle on their path, they gather their friends to go through it, under it or over it, never giving up until they reach their target.

Imagine... Yourself so determined that you never give in - you just adapt and change direction. What could you achieve if you joined with friends and worked on a big task tiny step by tiny step?

Affirm... I keep moving forward - with friends or alone - I never give up.

Ancestors

My ancestors are up above
They watch and understand
Supporting me in every way
They want to lend a hand

Power and strength they send to me
Each step and choice I make
Smiling as I work things out
And learn from each mistake

They know I am their legacy
I have been since my birth
Quietly they hold my hand
As I journey on the earth

Explore & Discover

Consider... Do you think your ancestors look down from above with judgment or with understanding? Could they have a clear view from their present position? Would they want their family line, their DNA to thrive here on earth?

Realise... We have many ancestors who came before us; we carry their genetic code. During their lives they always did their best with what they had available at that time. Now it is our time to do the same. We are the ones who are here struggling or dancing through the challenges of today. We are the legacy of those who went before. Our ancestors support and guide us towards success and happiness in their own unique ways.

Imagine... A campfire scene, make it feel really safe - you might like to take imaginary friends along for their support and protection (such as powerful animals or even angels). One by one invite your ancestors to come and share their wisdom with you.

Affirm... I am the one living and breathing - I am the legacy of those who came before me.

Listen

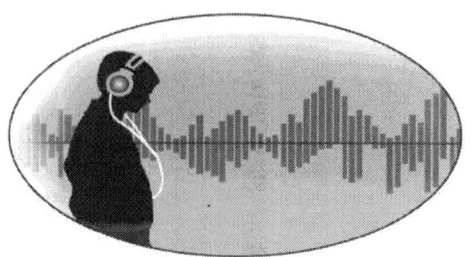

There's a voice on my shoulder
It always says no
It tells me to stop
When it's my time to go

It whispers to me
All its doubts and it's fears
And I have been listening
For too many years

From now all my thinking
Can be gentle and kind
Like a radio station
I will re-tune my mind

Explore & Discover

Consider... Do you have negative thoughts that are playing in the background of your life - like a depressing and judgmental radio station that sits on your shoulder and whispers in your ear? Is it possible that what it is saying is not true for you right now? How would your life be if you whispered positive things to yourself all day?

Realise... When a comment or thought makes an impact on us, we often remember it, burying it deeply in our unconscious mind. Most people store lots of judgmental comments that may not be true. Like a radio station running quietly in the background, we may not notice that we are whispering these thoughts and comments over and over to ourselves each day. Maybe we can retune the words to radio 'kind' - or even radio 'powerful'.

Imagine... Listening to the voice on your shoulder, and writing down its words. Slowly questioning the truth of what is being said, then rewriting its words into more positive and motivating statements.

Affirm... I am choosing my own thought beliefs and actions - all my thoughts are kind, powerful and positive today.

Heart Talk

Sometimes decisions
Are made from my head
I'm learning to listen
To my heart talk instead

When it is all quiet
There's a truth deep inside
It whispers of wisdom
It's a kind loving guide

I drop my attention
To the voice in my chest
I'm learning to trust it
As it always knows best

Explore & Discover

Consider... How do you make your decisions? Do you listen to other people, the voice on your shoulder or the one in your head? As a child you listened to your instinct, your gut, your heart, do you listen to that now? Would life be easier and more peaceful if you trusted your own inner guidance system, if you always knew what was really true and right for you?

Realise... We all have light bulb moments, moments when we just KNOW something is true - when we recognise something that we always knew somewhere deep inside. These are times when we connect to our inner wisdom, our gut instinct, the quiet, kind voice within our heart centre. When we ask questions focused on this area we become aware that we already knew so many of the answers.

Imagine... Sitting in silence, dropping your attention to the centre of your chest and asking a quiet, simple question - without any expectation of what the reply might be.

Affirm... I listen to my heart - I trust my own intuition to be my guide now.

Words

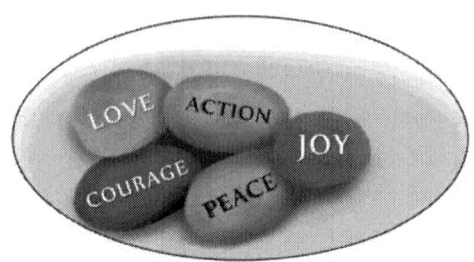

The words I use - the words I think
I choose them now with care
The quiet ones I whisper deep
Or those I speak and share

I've decided it is time
To put down doubt and fear
And focus on the things I want
With language loud and clear

I am choosing joy and peace
Each word sends out a call
My arms are open really wide
So I receive it all

Explore & Discover

Consider... Do you use more negative or positive words? Do you notice more negative or positive words in the media each day? What would happen if you always used positive words when talking to yourself or other people?

Realise... Words are the way we communicate within ourselves and with the outside world. Positive words carry a positive effect and vibration wherever they go. The affirmations (Affirm...) statements on these pages are positive, powerful, creative words. As you repeat them aloud, you send a loud, clear message into the world that this is what you believe. This is like a magnet and attracts more of what you are thinking or saying; it calls more of that vibration towards you.

Imagine... Sending out a clear call for peace, joy, power, love, acceptance, forgiveness (whatever you want to attract). Then open your arms and notice those positive words and ideas pouring in like colour or energy, flooding into every cell of your body.

Affirm... I choose positive words to create a positive life for myself right now.

My Truth

I have the courage
To say how I feel
I'll speak from my heart now
I am honest and real

I'm true to myself
I sing my own song
I'm completely determined
To keep calm and strong

Let the world stop and listen
From now I'll be heard
As loudly and clearly
I am sharing each word

Explore & Discover

Consider... How do you communicate what you are thinking to others? Do you hold it in and keep quiet? Do you sometimes hold so much in that it overflows unexpectedly in angry outbursts or backhanded comments? If you were a great communicator would you be heard and understood more often?

Realise... Communication is a skill to be learnt and practiced. If our parents did not know how to communicate well themselves, they could not teach us. Assertive communication is respectful and honours both parties, leading to better understanding and closer relationships. Other people never know exactly what we are feeling, or what we want, unless we tell them in a way that can be clearly heard.

Imagine... Deciding what point you would like to make, sitting down with someone, making eye contact, slowly repeating your point while keeping calm and strong. Feeling relieved, heard, adult and powerful, during and after the interaction.

Affirm... I am a calm, strong, confident communicator.

DNA

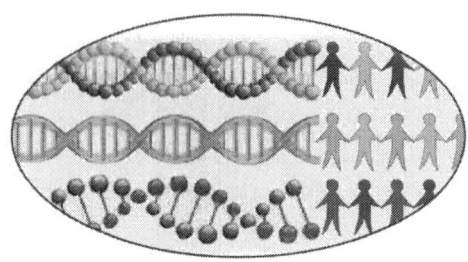

Everyone that lives and breaths
Is not the same as me
We do not think or look alike
That's our diversity

I'm not a clone I'm quite unique
It's in my DNA
And now I've come to realise
It's designed to be that way

I can't fit in - so I'll stand out
Courageous strong and free
Enjoy each moment that arrives
Be who I'm meant to be

Explore & Discover

Consider... Do you try hard to be like other people? Do you wish you were taller, thinner, had different hair or skin? How would you know who you are if everyone looked and sounded alike - if we were all identical? Do you try to fit in or celebrate standing out?

Realise... Many people aspire to look like models but never will. Many people wish they could live other people's lives and end up not really enjoying their own. It is part of humanity's design that we are all different or we would all be the same. The differences between us create an unlimited number of challenges and adventures. By noticing who we are not, we can realise who we really are as individuals. Our uniqueness is something to be valued and celebrated.

Imagine... A planet where everyone is a clone - where everyone looks and thinks exactly the same way. Then notice the Earth - our planet - this world where everyone looks, thinks and acts differently. Notice with wonder the intricate weaving of our DNA and our interwoven lives.

Affirm... I am unique and perfect as I am.

Water

I'm watching the water
From the hills to the sea
It never gives up
In its wish to be free

The stream does not worry
Does not need to know
In stillness or rapids
It goes with the flow

It slowly dissolves
Any blockage away
There's no one and nothing
That stands in its way

Explore & Discover

Consider… How do you move through life? If you were part of a stream would you be at the bottom in the dark or sparkling and dancing on the top? Would you be resting in pools or rushing so much that you do not notice your surroundings? Do you battle with life or accept what is happening and enjoy going with the flow?

Realise… That water knows where it is going - it is travelling on a journey from its source, wandering down to the sea, then cycling around and doing it all again. It is never stressed; it travels easily and quietly. It is an expert at going with the flow. When it meets an obstacle it goes around it, but slowly wears away any blockage with its simple persistence.

Imagine… Being like the water - you could choose to rush like rapids, float in pools or slow down to enjoy the view, moving in any way that suits you today. Imagine never being stressed by what is happening around you, as you happily go with the flow.

Affirm… I am enjoying my journey - I choose to go with the flow.

Peace

It's time to step out of the chaos
To stop and admire the view
Loving and living each moment
Find wonder in everything new

My life it is slowly unfolding
Each breath is a treasure so fine
I drop into gentle slow motion
As I savour each blessing that's mine

All of my senses are heightened
Awakening stillness in me
With peace and with light I'm surrounded
Now it's enough to just be

Explore & Discover

Consider... Do you spend time appreciating the precious moment of now? Do you step out of the chaos and choose stillness? Do you find time for silence and inner peace?

Realise... Sometimes life is like getting on a roller-coaster ride and not being able to reach the controls. We get so caught up in the doing that we do not get a chance just to be. We can choose to slow life down and consider the benefits of peace and quiet using meditation, energy balancing or spiritual practice. When we explore what is available we can find our own way to make a deeper connection to life, its source and ourselves.

Imagine... Stopping and closing your eyes, then walking down some steps, deeper and deeper into relaxation. Allow your amazing imagination to focus on creating a peaceful place that is perfect for you, such as a garden or beach. Sit there for a while and then return up the steps into full awareness. Do this regularly and let it become a new habit.

Affirm... I am stopping to find the peace within me.

Waking

Freedom is mine every morning
I wake and I open my eyes
A new day is here with its dawning
Each moment a perfect surprise

I notice that my heart is beating
I'm grateful for each breath I take
Look how my body is moving
It follows each thought that I make

My past and my future don't matter
I'm moving them out of my way
I love and I live without limits
My power and choice is today

Explore & Discover

Consider... Do you greet each morning as the first day of the rest of your life? Do you recognise all the choices that appear with each new day's arrival?

Realise... Every morning when we wake and realise we are still alive, we have so much to celebrate. We have ahead of us another day when we can choose what we do and how we live. We may have many habits and addictions but we can choose to leave those all behind us in the past. This really is the first day of the rest of our lives, so every moment is a blessing to be enjoyed and savoured. This is a special time. There is a great call going out to humanity - to those who have been sleepwalking - to wake up, to make a difference in the evolution of mankind. Every thought and action matters now. Every positive step we take, every positive word we use, is helping to raise the vibration of this planet.

Imagine... Waking as if this was your first or your last day on earth. What would you do differently today? What would you say to yourself?

Affirm... I am here and I am fully awake right now.

Connecting

My arms and my heart they are open
I celebrate each breath I take
With life and with love I'm connecting
Now I am here and awake

I let go of all expectations
There's nothing to judge or to fear
I drop into wonder and wisdom
Enjoying each moment that's here

All of my boundaries dissolving
I can surrender and fall
Watching perfection unfolding
Now I am one with it all

Explore & Discover

Consider... Are your arms and your heart open or closed? Do you sometimes feel disconnected or lonely? Do you have your own spiritual beliefs? Do you have a connection with the source of life? Would you like to know for certain that you are always supported, safe and never alone?

Realise... Many of our ancestors had a routine of daily spiritual practice. Traditionally this was through one of the established religions, but now many people are stepping out of those boxes and awakening to many more choices and possibilities. When we are ready to make a deep connection to something powerful and loving there are many external and internal options to explore. This journey of exploration is full of amazing experiences; the destination is boundless peace, trust and wonder.

Imagine... Letting go of the struggle and KNOWING you are never alone. Always feeling supported, guided and connected to everything.

Affirm... I am surrounded by invisible friends, who always understand - I am never alone.

Armour

When I do not feel safe
I put up my guard
A shield of protection
Which is shiny and hard

But this is too heavy
It keeps others away
This whole suit of armour
I know it can't stay

I believe I can cope
I have power inside
I am strong and protected
I will no longer hide

Explore & Discover

Consider... Do you wear invisible armour to keep yourself safe? Does this keep others out or keep you trapped inside? Could there be an easier way to feel safe? Would you feel safer and stronger if only positive thoughts, comments and energies could reach you today?

Realise... To avoid hurt or negative energy we often make a protective, invisible boundary to keep others out. Sometimes it is like heavy armour which keeps everything and everyone away. We can take this off and replace it with an imaginary bubble of light and energy, which can protect us in a similar way. This allows compliments, gifts, positive people and energy to reach us much more easily.

Imagine... Taking off your heavy armour for a while and choosing to replace it with a bubble of light. Allow the outer edge to be a filter, which allows only good and positive energies to reach you - so everything else bounces off. Add layers of colour on the outside until it feels strong. Explore how well it works by imagining wearing it in stressful situations.

Affirm... I am safe and protected in my bubble of light.

Ripples

From a pebble dropped in water
Waves move across the pond
With energy and light
They spread out far beyond

Everything I'm choosing
It ripples out from me
Sharing thoughts and actions
With friends and family

When feeling love or anger
It flows from deep inside
Expanding out beyond me
It travels far and wide

Explore & Discover

Consider... Our thoughts, feelings and energy always spread outwards, touching the people around us. What kind of vibrations are you sharing today? What positive thoughts or feelings would you like to pass on to the people closest to you?

Realise... Ideas and moods can be infectious; they can spread from person to person. When we are around negative people, we can soon become negative ourselves; their mood can lower our mood. The opposite is true when we are with happy or positive people. How we feel spreads like ripples in water. In each moment we are dropping our own pebble in the centre of an ever-expanding circle.

Imagine... One person who is completely relaxed, comfortable and confident within themselves. Notice the energy of their joy and happiness spreading to their friends and family, then rippling out into their community and flowing out into the world.

Affirm... I am filling my body and mind with positive, loving thoughts today - then letting them overflow and spread out into my world.

Footprints

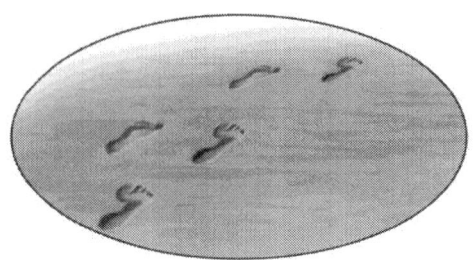

I place my mark upon the world
With thought, with hand, with shoe
A trail of steps and energy
That's formed by what I do

Every action that I take
Everywhere I've been
The weight I place upon the earth
Like footprints can be seen

Remember me for what I've done
And let your thoughts be kind
Please know that I have done my best
To leave some good behind

Explore & Discover

Consider... What impact have you left upon the earth and other people with your actions? What legacy will you leave behind when you leave this planet? Have you made a positive difference to other people's lives? Are there footprints you would still like to make?

Realise... We choose our own actions based on our present beliefs and thinking. Our thoughts focus our physical bodies to use specific force and energy to impact on the physical objects or living things in our world. While we live and breathe we can always make new footprints, we can make a new impression and create a new legacy. When we support others, when we are kind, generous and loving, we are creating the most amazing and long remembered footprints of all.

Imagine... Noticing your past achievements, then considering what other footprints you would like to leave behind on this planet.

Affirm... Today I chose actions that will leave some good behind.

Party

I'm present on the earth
It's where I'm meant to be
I lift a glass and celebrate
The joy of being me

Every step I'm taking
I leave behind more fears
So here's to life and living
For I am saying cheers

Let's all have a party
A new day has begun
Let's drink to love and laughter
It's time to have some fun

Explore & Discover

Consider... When did you last have a really good party to celebrate something? Do you celebrate life? Do you celebrate who you are and what you have achieved? How much fun and laughter do you allow into your world?

Realise... Living on the earth is not supposed to be hard - it is supposed to be a playground for great adventures and new experiences. When we stop to notice, we become aware of all our gifts and blessings. We can choose to celebrate any of these - a friend, family member, arrival, departure, event, achievement, discovery, etc., etc. We can have a private or public party for anything we are happy about. We can make life a little bit of fun, lots of fun or a party every day.

Imagine... Choosing something (small or large) that is worth celebrating today, then finding your own way to celebrate it. Turn up the fun and excitement of today and celebrate life.

Affirm... I have so much to celebrate - I am choosing fun, laughter and joy right now.

Take a new direction
Your dreams they wait for you
It takes a little action
To make them all come true

The Toolbox

To take things to pieces
Or create something new
We all work with tools
Whatever we do

The ones in this toolbox
Are easy to use
So pick one and try it
You have nothing to lose

With time and some practice
Your life will improve
So put in some effort
And make a new groove

Using the Toolbox

To change our home or car we often use tools; they make the job easier, quicker and often more enjoyable. We can improve or repair any part of our outer world when we have the right tools for the job. Often when we use a new tool for the first time it seems strange and awkward to work with - however with practice, we soon build up our confidence. Sometimes we discover that a tool is such good fun we might find ourselves looking around for more things to make or repair just so that we can carry on being creative and using our exciting new toy.

This is a different kind of toolbox; it is for making changes to our inner world rather than our outer one. Redecorating our home may bring us brief joy, but with enough positive thoughts and feelings inside us, we can experience that joy every moment of every day, whatever is happening around us.

The content of this unique toolbox, combined with the rhymes and their opposing pages, allow you to use every word in this book as a tool for your growth and development.

By reading this book you are showing that you are ready for change. Maybe you have noticed that you have been going round and round in circles, maybe you have become locked into cycles of inactivity and stagnation. Maybe this is your time to grow, to expand, to adapt, to realign whatever is not working for you. Maybe all you need is the right guidance or tools to get creative and make some positive changes in your life.

Whatever emotional or practical changes you decide to make, these tools will make your work easier. If you leave them in the toolbox then they cannot work for you, only applying them will make things happen in your life.

The changes will happen as fast as you can handle them. Maybe you want to tread carefully and explore change gently; maybe it is time for some big changes so you can reach happiness and freedom more quickly. Each hour that you invest in using them will bring its own result and rewards.

With such an amazing selection of new tools at your disposal you can enjoy sorting through them, taking a few out of the box and finding out which ones you enjoy using. Have fun experimenting with them, discovering which ones bring you the deepest, most wonderful, lasting outcomes.

Guidelines

This advice is intended to make your work with the tools easier and deeper, giving you more effortless and rewarding results.

Whenever the exercise allows it: close your eyes to listen to your own intuition and inner wisdom. It is easier to know what is true for you when your eyes are closed and you focus within your own body, particularly in the centre of your chest.

Say things aloud: Our voice takes our hidden inner thoughts and releases them into our outer world where we can really hear and notice what we are saying. Speak what you are doing aloud whenever you can.

Take action: When you notice an opportunity to change your actions for the better, take it. As you alter your thought processes and beliefs, changes in your behaviour will naturally follow. If you believe you are free, your actions will become less limited and more curious and confident.

Appreciate your efforts: It is important to value your achievements, to find a way to turn up the praise and pat yourself on the back. You might enjoy creating a star chart to record your efforts or results. You might want to write and reread what you have discovered, so you can notice what you have learnt, how much you have grown and moved forward.

Be gentle with the others: The people around you may not realise why or how you have changed; they may be comfortable with their old routines. Your changes may be greeted with enthusiasm or they might confuse people close to you. Give partners, friends and family time and space to adapt, to find their own way to come back into balance, as you make the changes that are right for you.

Preparation

Whether we are putting up shelves or preparing a meal, before we start any task, we decide what we want to achieve with our time and energy. Then we make sure we have set aside time, are in the right environment and have ingredients or tools available to work with. If you are serious about making some changes then there are a few things to consider before you begin.

Find a regular time: Set aside some one hour slots, several times a week, allow this to become part of your weekly routine. You might find it useful to write down set times in your diary or set an alarm on your phone until these patterns are established. Remember, everything gets easier and more comfortable with practice.

Choose a calm place: Your environment is important, so find somewhere safe, quiet and relaxing, away from the chaos of your outer world. Maybe light a candle to make it calm and special for yourself.

Get your equipment ready: Treat yourself to some notebooks and pens that are bright and inviting. Select a small notebook (A3 or smaller) to carry with you, helping you to keep your focus on what you are learning. Having an A5 notebook will allow you to write freely, recording each discovery and breakthrough. Rereading your own book of wisdom in the future can be very rewarding, as it allows you to notice how much you have learnt and grown

Get excited: Dare to dream of the results these tools can bring you. Daydream about how you want your life to be in six months, or in five years.
Choose an attitude of excitement each time you set off to explore your inner world, remembering that these are your steps towards happiness and freedom. Release the playful and curious child within that wants to push at the boundaries; allow yourself to enjoy each new moment of wonder and discovery.

Have a brainstorming session: Set some goals. Begin this by writing down anything you would like to achieve in the next week, month or year. You might want to choose a goal for some of these areas: home, health, relationships, work, family, friendships, hobbies, money, fun or adventures. Once you have written them down, take time to imagine them coming true.

Make your goals achievable and remember they are just points to aim for, just dreams to pull you forward. They cannot be set in stone; writing them in pencil will allow you to return and rewrite them, adapting your personal targets as you change and grow.

NOTES

....
....
....
....
....
....
....
....
....
....
....
....
....

If there's something to re-wire
Or you've noticed a loose screw
It might be time to fix it
With a tool that's right for you

Using the Rhymes

The rhymes themselves are tools for change; they can assist in many ways as you take each step towards freedom. The first ideas offered here are to be used in combination with the rhymes, suggesting new and exciting ways to enhance your usual reading of them. Like any tool, more practice will lead to more effective results. If you use them a little, they will have a small effect; if you use them regularly and with commitment, they will slowly but steadily make a positive change on your thinking and your life.

Choose them

There are 52 rhymes on the subject of freedom in this book, allowing you to choose a different one each week for a year - if you prefer a slower pace then you could easily select one rhyme per fortnight or per month. Remember that there is no right or wrong way to use them. The time and effort you put in will produce the results that follow.

Begin by going through the book and finding one rhyme that pleases you, resonates with you or just feels right for you today.

Choose to focus on it for at least a week. Have fun with the variety of techniques available below, selecting ones that allow you to learn and absorb a rhyme's message and its positive, powerful words.

Read them

Reading the rhyme over and over again allows you to memorise it in the same way that you may have learnt the words to nursery rhymes or your times tables. Choose a time when you are relaxed and calm. This allows you to be more receptive to the ideas and words. It could be when you wake early in the morning or when you are resting before going to sleep. If you have already established personal reflection or quiet time, you can read them as part of your regular spiritual practice, prayer or mediation.

Write them

Write your chosen rhyme and then place it where you can look at it regularly, maybe on a wall or the fridge. This will allow the rhyme's words to stay with you, whatever you are doing throughout your day. You might want to laminate a copy for your pocket or write the rhyme into your small notebook or diary. Have fun with your amazing imagination and get creative with how and where you write your rhyme.

Say them
Saying the rhyme aloud and with feeling will allow it to come into your body through the sense of your hearing. This is how much of your original core programming and learning arrived, so this adds weight and power to the words. You could also record the rhymes onto your phone, laptop or MP3 player, and then listen to the recordings.

Sing them
Singing a rhyme is a great way to learn it - it gives you an opportunity to combine your musical and creative imagination with the words of the rhymes. You can have fun playing with the rhythm and words, or even adapting the phrases to fit a chosen tune. You may be surprised by how quickly you will learn a rhyme and how deeply you will absorb its message when you sing it rather than read or say it.

Sit with them
This tool is gentle, yet powerful. You will gain the most from using when you have at least 30 minutes of quiet time to complete it. Doing this exercise allows you to stop and consider the truth of what you think and believe. With it, you can listen to your own heart, connect with your own inner source of wisdom and find out what is really true for you.

Begin by slowly and carefully selecting one or two positive lines from a rhyme, or even choosing an 'affirm' statement that appeals to you. You might want to select a phrase or idea you would really like to believe, but cannot accept, as it conflicts with your present thinking on the subject. Write down your chosen phrase so you can repeat it over and over again. Remember that there is no guarantee that the words you have chosen are true and accurate; there is no guarantee that they are not. The idea of this tool is to allow you to focus within, adapt old thinking and discover your own truth.

- Find a quiet, peaceful space and make yourself comfortable.
- Slowly and carefully say your chosen phrase aloud and with feeling.
- Close your eyes.
- Take in some deep breaths and allow yourself to relax.
- Focus on your heart area - the centre of your chest - as you slowly, quietly, gently repeat the same phrase aloud several times.

- Notice any tension in your body and focus your attention on it as you slowly, quietly, gently repeat the same phrase aloud several times.

- Gently, softly, patiently, quietly sit with the words as the truth is revealed to you.

- You may feel emotional as your old thinking adjusts to this new idea - welcome any emotional releases. If you feel angry then feel free to rant. If you feel tearful then feel free to cry. Release your emotions from where they have been held for so long, allowing them to come up and out as you slowly, quietly, gently repeat the same phrase aloud over and over to yourself.

- Allow your body and your mind to go through all of its tension until you reach the peace and calm that lies beyond it (you will know when everything goes calm and still) as you slowly, quietly, gently repeat the same phrase aloud over and over to yourself.

- Eventually you will absolutely know what is true for you. You will notice how well everything falls into place, how good it feels, how well it fits. You will have made a connection with your own truth and your inner wisdom. You will discover that so many answers were always inside you, waiting to be heard; they just needed an opportunity, such as this one, for you to become aware of them.

- One phrase every few days may be enough deep change for your system. Please be gentle with yourself, resting well and drinking plenty of spring water, as there may be adjustments going on in your mind and body for several days following this exercise.

- A few days later, slowly, quietly, gently repeat the same phrase aloud to yourself - you will experience it very differently

Live them

Choose a rhyme and try living it one day at a time; When you wake in the morning, choose a rhyme for the day and read it several times. If you are facing a particular challenge that day you might want to choose one that may help you through it. Daydream and imagine what you could do differently if you completely accepted the words of the rhyme, if you believed it, if you knew it was true.

Use your imagination to select anything you can really, practically, physically do differently today with these new ideas in your mind. Rehearse your new ideas and choices in your head, then have the courage and confidence to take them from your head and really make them happen.

As you adapt your own behaviour in this way, you demonstrate to yourself that change is possible. You will soon discover that you are developing the skill and flexibility to make the changes more easily, to wake with each dawn, take back control of your life and choose positive, powerful, free thoughts and actions.

Share them
Share the rhymes with the people you meet, letting them spread like pebbles dropped into water, sending little waves of positive energy from person to person. Pass on a rhyme; print one out and share it (please put the book title or website address on the printed page). Offer your discoveries gently and kindly, with no expectation of what other people will say or do in response. Give them what you have to offer and let it go. Let those who receive your open-hearted gifts use them in their own way, to make the changes they are ready to make.

Although we are all different, there are many like-minded people who are interested in all aspects of self-development. At this time many people are asking the same types of questions and searching for the same kinds of answers. It is now possible to gather with others to share what you are discovering. You may be able to join a group or start one of your own.

The rhymes and the ideas behind them offer wonderful material for the subject of a group discussion or personal development course. There are details of how to run or join a local rhymes group on the following website:

www.rhymesoflife.info

Discovering More

The next set of tools are intended to be combined with the 'Explore & Discover' pages, which accompany each of the 52 rhymes. Each heading here has the same title and relates directly to the four sections on those pages.

Consider...

These sections of the 'Explore & Discover' pages ask you to question what you think and believe in a new way. Our own answers come more easily when we are asked to consider gentle and empowering questions. While reading these sections you may find it useful to stop, reflect and think for a while. Sit quietly, focus on the centre of your chest and wait for your own answers to come. You might like to write down your discoveries in your A5 notebook. Going through these notes with a highlighting pen allows you to select your own pearls of wisdom, create your own affirmations and add them to the small book of positive phrases you now choose to carry with you.

Sharing a question with a friend or in a self-development group is also an option - sometimes two heads are better than one, and you can get new perspectives by listening to the opinions of others.

Remember that we are all individuals so others will have their own unique viewpoint on the question or the answer. Just reflect on their opinion, then focus on the centre of your chest and trust your own 'gut' feelings, your own instinct and inner knowing. With practice, focusing within for your answers becomes easier and easier, as you become more 'centred' and learn to trust what, on some level of your being, you always knew.

Recognise...

Each idea put forward in this section of the 'Explore & Discover' pages offers new perspectives and views on life. Suggesting ways to put down some old ideas and pick up some new, healthier and more balanced ways to understand the world. Remember to use your own judgment about what you accept and take from these ideas on each of the different aspects of freedom.

You may find it useful to set aside time to read these words slowly and carefully; the more you repeat them, especially aloud, the more easily they will be absorbed and accepted into your heart and mind.

You may discover that what you were taught as a child was not always the whole truth. You may realise that some of these positive, empowering words just feel right and true; you *know* them, you recognise them. Each light bulb moment of wonder and discovery can be like finding a long-lost friend, someone you once knew but had forgotten. These revelations often just seem to fit; as somehow we recognise the deep and meaningful truth of the words. You may want to record what you notice in your own book of wisdom.

Imagine...

In this section of the 'Explore & Discover' pages you are invited to use your amazing imagination. Our imagination can be a great way to explore new paths and ideas that we have never fully considered. We sometimes use our imaginations to project our worries and fears into the future believing that this will keep us safe, but here we are invited to use our imaginations in a much more productive and creative way. When our imagination is occupied with lovely daydreams full of new possibilities, it cannot also spend time worrying. With a little practice the future soon appears much more hopeful, more positive, interesting and inviting.

What you are encouraged to imagine varies with the subject of the rhyme and its message. Whether you are invited to imagine breathing something in, writing something down or a dreamy possible future, you can still set aside time for imagining. You do not need to visualise it; you might find it easier to hear it, feel it or just know it is happening. Every positive trip you take into your own wisdom in this way is like a rehearsal, it opens doors to amazing new opportunities and possibilities.

When you have selected something to imagine from the 'Explore & Discover' pages, find a quiet time and place for contemplation, close your eyes and focus on your chest, take in a few deep breaths, then set your wonderful imagination free. Imagine yourself right inside that experience; see what you can see, hear what you can hear, feel what you can feel and even add smells and other sensations.

Release your childlike sense of wonder and enthusiasm, make everything colourful, bright and inviting. Make all your imaginings perfect for you; the more you use your senses within the experience, the more real the experience will become for you. Remember, there are no limits on what is possible when you enter your own glorious world of pure imagination.

Affirm...

These sections of the 'Explore & Discover' pages usually contain one simple positive phrase - this is called an 'affirmation'. We are all affirming things all the time; our self-talk is the words we whisper quietly to ourselves. For many people, this self-talk is negative or judgmental, as if they had someone sitting on their shoulder, telling them what they cannot or should not do. Sometimes it is like listening to a radio station that has always played negative music; eventually we have learnt the songs and started to sing along to them, so our thinking has also become negative.

Each affirmative statement opposite a rhyme gives you one simple, positive thought. With these positive affirmations you can choose to retune your thinking, consciously choosing the words, ideas or self-talk that you want to hear. You can choose powerful, free thoughts that you want to believe and repeat them until they replace old thinking and programming.

Affirmative statements (or affirmations) are always set in the present - as though they have already happened. They may seem strange at first but are written in this way to write over the phrases that we usually say to ourselves.

For example, if you usually say to yourself, 'I can't do it myself', then a good affirmation to use would be, 'I can do it myself'. If the voice on your shoulder whispers, 'I am stupid', then a useful affirmation to choose would be, 'I am bright - and still learning something new each day'. You can use the affirmations in this book, or get creative and make some of your own.

To use the 'affirm' statements, select one you would like to believe and then:

- Repeat it aloud.
- Repeat it with belief and conviction in your voice.
- Repeat it at a regular time during your day.
- Write it in your small notebook or laminate it to carry with you

If you wish to use affirmations to focus on another theme rather than personal freedom, there are many, many more affirmations on subjects such as relationships or wealth on the internet. Give yourself time to select them, repeat them, learn them and accept them. Learn to trust your own gut feeling, your own inner knowing, your amazingly wise and perfect heart.

A Final Message

I believe you can
Make all your dreams come true
I want to let you know
That I believe in you

I hope you find a way
To let yourself be free
To take off all the limits
Be all that you can be

Keep on moving forward
In truth you'll find release
It is worth all the effort
To live in joy and peace

NOTES

Made in the USA
Charleston, SC
24 January 2014